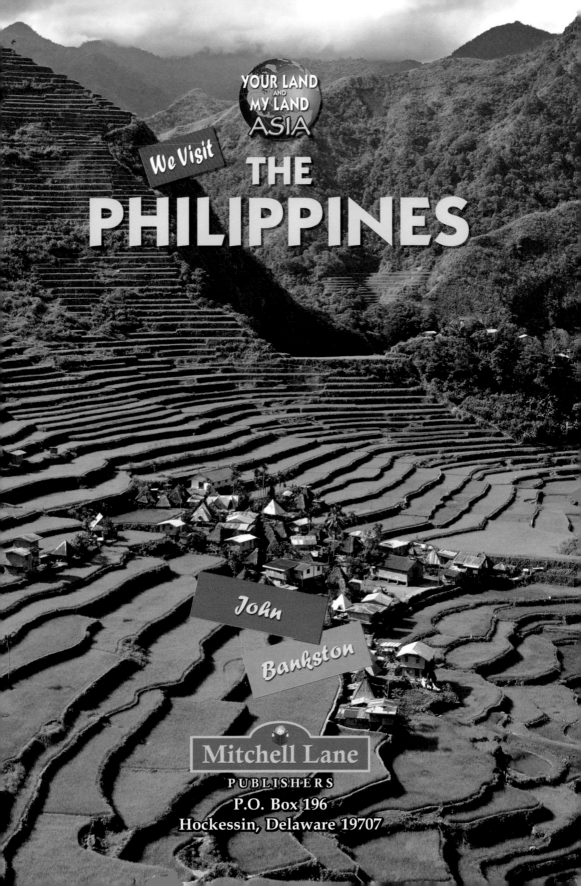

YOUR LAND
AND
MY LAND
ASIA

We Visit

THE
PHILIPPINES

John

Bankston

Mitchell Lane

PUBLISHERS
P.O. Box 196
Hockessin, Delaware 19707

YOUR LAND
AND
MY LAND
ASIA

Cambodia
China
India
Indonesia
Japan
Malaysia
North Korea
The Philippines
Singapore
South Korea

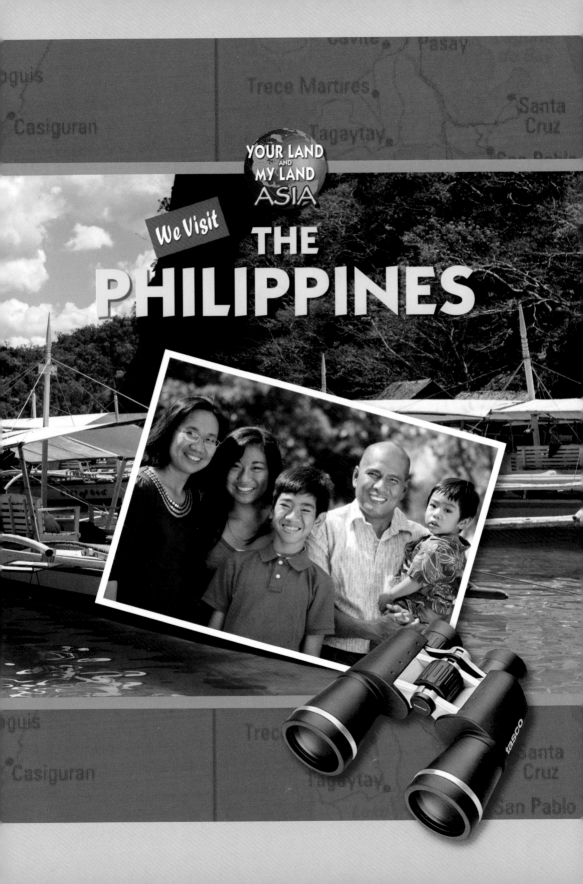

YOUR LAND
AND
MY LAND
ASIA

We Visit

THE
PHILIPPINES

Mitchell Lane

PUBLISHERS

Printing   1   2   3   4   5   6   7   8   9

Asia

Library of Congress Cataloging-in-Publication Data
Bankston, John, 1974–
    We visit the Philippines / by John Bankston.
        pages cm. — (Your land and my land: Asia)
    Includes bibliographical references and index.
    ISBN 978-1-61228-483-5 (library bound)
    1. Philippines—Juvenile literature. I. Title.
    DS655.B35 2013
    959.9—dc23
                                                2013033977
eBook ISBN: 9781612285382

Contents

Introduction

Stretching like a hook pointed toward Australia, the Philippines is a country of islands lying at the eastern edge of Southeast Asia. In addition to the Philippines, Southeast Asia includes Myanmar (formerly known as Burma), Malaysia, Thailand, Cambodia, Laos, and Vietnam, along with the island nations of Singapore, Brunei, Indonesia, and East Timor.

It is part of a region dominated by an archipelago—a stretch of water containing many islands. Known as the Malay Archipelago or the East Indian Archipelago, it is over 4,000 miles (6,440 kilometers) long from east to west and about 1,300 miles (2,100 kilometers) wide from north to south. It is the largest archipelago in the world. Lying between the Asian mainland and Australia, it includes Indonesia and the Philippines, along with some 25,000 islands.

Like most countries in Southeast Asia, the Philippines was once a colony. Its people were governed by distant rulers in Spain for more than 350 years. In 1898, however, the country was taken over by the United States. Nearly 50 years later, in the aftermath of World War II and a short-lived Japanese occupation, the Philippines finally became a free and independent nation.

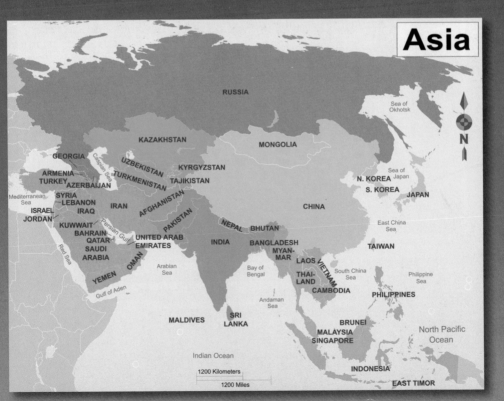

The Philippines is an island nation. Most of the islands are fairly similar, with sandy shorelines and hills like these Chocolate Hills of Bohol further inland.

Asia

RUSSIA

KAZAKHSTAN

MONGOLIA

Sea of Okhotsk

GEORGIA

ARMENIA
TURKEY
AZERBAIJAN

Caspian Sea

UZBEKISTAN

KYRGYZSTAN

TURKMENISTAN
TAJIKISTAN

Sea of Japan

N. KOREA
S. KOREA

JAPAN

Mediterranean Sea

SYRIA
LEBANON
ISRAEL
JORDAN
IRAQ

IRAN

AFGHANISTAN

CHINA

East China Sea

KUWWAIT
BAHRAIN
QATAR
SAUDI
ARABIA

Persian Gulf

PAKISTAN

NEPAL
BHUTAN

Red Sea

UNITED ARAB
EMIRATES

OMAN

INDIA

BANGLADESH

MYAN-
MAR

TAIWAN

YEMEN

Gulf of Aden

Arabian
Sea

Bay of
Bengal

LAOS
THAI-
LAND

VIETNAM

South China
Sea

Philippine
Sea

CAMBODIA

PHILIPPINES

Andaman
Sea

MALDIVES

SRI
LANKA

BRUNEI

North Pacific
Ocean

MALAYSIA
SINGAPORE

Indian Ocean

1200 Kilometers

1200 Miles

INDONESIA

EAST TIMOR

N

Many people in the Philippines live and work in crowded high-rise condos and office parks such as the Rockwell section of Manila's Makati City.

Chapter 1

The Philippines Overview

Welcome to the Philippines. If you've ever imagined living on a deserted island, this country could be ideal. Although the Philippines is made up of over 7,000 islands, less than 1,000 of them are inhabited. That means fewer than 15% have any people living on them at all. Some 95% of the country's population lives on just 11 of the largest islands. If the islands of the Philippines were pushed together, their land area would be about the size of Nevada.

Geographers divide the Philippines into three groups of islands. The southern group includes Mindanao and the Sulu Archipelago. The majority of the country's islands are in the central group, called the Visayas. Its major islands include Bohol, Cebu, Leyte, Negros, Panay, and Samar. The northern group includes Luzon, the largest island. Luzon is also the site of Metropolitan Manila. Made up of 16 separate cities, including Manila—the country's capital—and Quezon City (its largest city), Metro Manila is home to nearly 12 million people.

The Philippines is actually the fastest growing country in Southeast Asia. Its population increased from 75 million in 2000 to almost 100 million in 2010. As of 2012, the median age in the Philippines was 23. That means that half the people are younger than 23, and half older. Across the Philippines, over 170 different dialects are spoken by a wide variety of ethnic groups.

A growing population means a greater demand for food, housing and other essentials. It can be challenging to provide these needs. Still, the Philippines is blessed with many natural resources.

With a warm, tropical climate, the country receives plenty of rain. Most daytime temperatures climb over 80°F (27°C). These conditions are ideal for growing crops such as sugarcane, rice, pineapples, bananas, and mangos. In spite of their increasing numbers, Filipinos don't eat all the fruit they grow. Instead they export the excess to other countries. This is a primary source of money for the Philippines. Besides fruit, the Philippines also exports tobacco, copper, gold, and a rope-making product known as abacá.

Islands are actually mountains, with most of the land lying below the ocean's surface. Most islands in the Philippines have similar features. Sandy beaches stretch along the shoreline, interrupted by bays and natural harbors. Further inland lie dense, tropical rainforests. Closer to the center of most islands are hills and mountains. Luzon is home to the Cordillera Central Range, where some peaks reach 9,000 feet (2,750 meters). Mount Apo, the country's tallest peak, is located on Mindanao and towers 9,692 feet (2,954 meters). Like many of the mountains in the Philippines, Mount Apo is an active volcano. The Philippines is within the "Ring of Fire." This is a horseshoe-shaped area some 25,000 miles long (40,000 kilometers) that extends completely

Many areas have remained untouched by development, like the pristine El Nido on Palawan.

FYI FACT:

In 1935, Charles Richter, a scientist who studied earthquakes, developed a system to indicate their strength. The Richter Scale shows the amount of energy released by an earthquake. Each number on the scale shows ground motion ten times greater than the number below it. A magnitude 5 means the ground motion is ten times greater than magnitude 4. Earthquakes over 7 are considered very dangerous and destructive.

around the rim of the Pacific Ocean from New Zealand to Chile. Over 90% of the world's earthquakes occur within the Ring of Fire, along with most of the world's volcanic eruptions. The Philippines suffers from both.

Although the Philippines has several minor earthquakes and volcanic eruptions each year, the early 1990s were particularly deadly. On July 16, 1990 a 7.7 magnitude earthquake centered in Luzon caused widespread

Scuba divers and snorkelers view breathtaking sea life, like these clownfish swimming alongside windflowers.

destruction and killed 1,621 people. Every February since then, the town of Baguio—the summer capital of the Philippines—has put on the Panagbenga Festival to celebrate the town's many flowers and symbolize its rebuilding after the earthquake. It includes a parade with floats made out of flowers and street dancers dressed in flowers. As newspaper reporter Edu Jarque observes, "There were flowers and more flowers—name it, and it was represented. I recall seeing roses of different hues, milflores whose sheer size amazed everyone, birds of paradise, carnations, and golden mums, anthuriums, and geraniums, vandas and dendrobiums, orchids from phalaenopsis to cattleyas."[1]

The next year, on June 15th, Luzon's Mount Pinatubo erupted for the first time in over 400 years. It was one of the most violent eruptions anywhere in the world in the 20th century. A series of eruptions over a period of several days spewed volcanic ash 22 miles (35 kilometers) in the air and hundreds of people died. Clark Air Base, established by the U.S. military in 1903, was damaged so badly that it was turned over to the Philippines. The eruption even had an effect on the Earth's climate. "It's a cooler world, thanks to Mt. Pinatubo," according to *Science News*. "Mt. Pinatubo ejected an estimated 20 million tons of sulfur dioxide gas into the stratosphere, where it formed tiny droplets of sulfuric acid. Such droplets, or aerosols, remain suspended in the upper atmosphere for several years following an eruption. Mt. Pinatubo's aerosol cloud, which circled the globe within a few weeks

The Philippine people celebrate a rich variety of ethnic backgrounds with traditions such as the annual Panagbenga Flower Festival in Baguio City on Luzon Island. Costumes include woven skirts known as tapis for women, while men wear bahags, or loincloths.

of its emergence, led scientists to speculate that incoming sunlight might be scattered or blocked, resulting in cooler temperatures on the ground."[2] The following year the speculation was confirmed. Temperatures in some places were nearly two degrees cooler than they would otherwise have been.

Over time, layers of volcanic ash form a mineral-rich soil. This is another reason, along with the climate, for the country's agricultural success. Only about one-third of the country's land is used for farming, yet it produces enough to feed the population and provide generous exports. Even on hilly land, farmers carve terraces where they can grow rice, a primary staple for many people in the country. In many parts of the Philippines, people plant and harvest the crops as they have for hundreds of years—by hand, with the help of a plow pulled by a carabao, a type of water buffalo.

Often called the national animal, the carabao is just one of many unusual creatures that live in and around the Philippine Islands. Nearly 200 species of mammals live in the Philippines. Some exist

The deadly Mount Pinatubo eruption in 1991 altered the world's climate, killed hundreds of people, and heavily damaged Clark Air Base, from where this photo was taken.

nowhere else on earth. Because people have developed the habitats these animals call home, many of them are endangered.

Although similar species exist across Asia, the Visayan spotted deer roams freely on only three islands in the Philippines. Less than 3,000 exist, and photos of them in the wild are extremely rare. Like many animals in the Philippines, it is nocturnal, preferring to eat at night. The nocturnal tarsier is related to the monkey. This small primate has huge eyes, a tiny body and very long hind limbs that look similar to a frog's. On the island of Bohol, the Philippine Tarsier and Wildlife Sanctuary lets visitors not only see the animals but also hold them in their hands!

The tiny deer mouse and the leopard cat are among many other endangered animals on the Philippines. Although the Philippines was once covered by forests, over the past century many of the trees have been cut down to make more room for people and farms. Just like in many countries, young people often leave small towns and villages to work in cities. They spend their adulthood living very close to others. Thousands of years ago, the population was spread out. The people who settled on the islands had little contact with anyone beyond the shoreline.

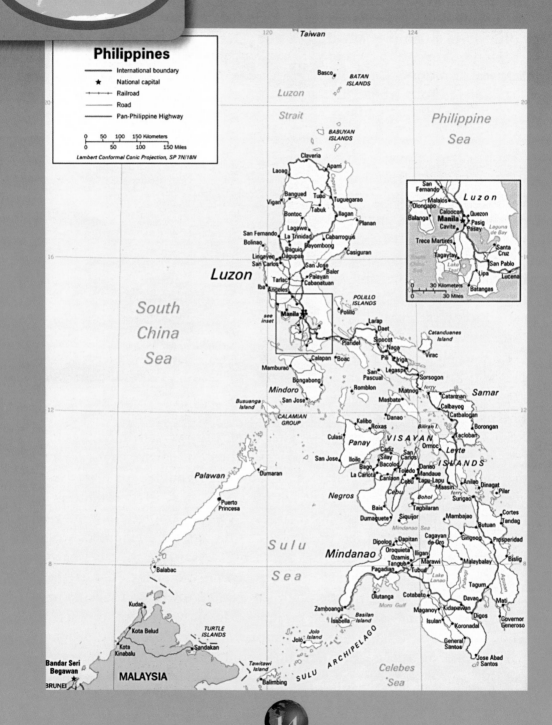

Where in the World

Philippines

- International boundary
- ★ National capital
- Railroad
- Road
- Pan-Philippine Highway

0 50 100 150 Kilometers
0 50 100 150 Miles

Lambert Conformal Conic Projection, SP 7N/18N

THE PHILIPPINES FACTS AT A GLANCE

Official Country Name: Republic of the Philippines

Official Language: Filipino and English; eight major dialects—Tagalog, Cebuano, Ilocano, Hiligaynon or Ilonggo, Bicol, Waray, Pampango, and Pangasinan

Population: 103,775,002 (July 2012 est.)

Land Area: 115,600 square miles (300,000 square km), slightly larger than Arizona

Capital: Manila

Government: Republic

Ethnic Makeup: Tagalog 28.1%, Cebuano 13.1%, Ilocano 9%, Bisaya/Binisaya 7.6%, Hiligaynon Ilonggo 7.5%, Bikol 6%, Waray 3.4%, other 25.3%

Religions: Catholic 82.9%, Islam 5%, Evangelical 2.8%, Iglesia ni Kristo 2.3%, other Christian 4.5%, other 1.8%, unspecified 0.6%, none 0.1% (2000 census)

Exports: semiconductors and electronic products, transportation equipment, garments, copper products, petroleum products, coconut oil, fruits

Imports: rice, electronic products, mineral fuels, machinery and transport equipment, iron and steel, textile fabrics, grains, chemicals, plastic

Crops: sugarcane, coconuts, rice, corn, bananas, cassavas, pineapples, mangoes; pork, eggs, beef; fish

Average Temperature: 80°F (27°C)

Average Annual Rainfall: 100 inches (254 cm)

Highest Point: Mount Apo 9,692 feet (2,954 meters)

Lowest Point: Philippine Sea (sea level)

Longest River: Cagayan River on Mindanao, 314 miles (505 km)

National Flag: Adopted in 1898, the flag of the Philippines has two equal horizontal bands of blue and red, with a white equilateral triangle on the hoist side. Blue stands for peace and justice, while red symbolizes courage. The flag flies with the blue side up in times of peace and the red side up in wartime. The white triangle represents equality; the eight rays recall the first eight provinces that sought independence from Spain. Each corner contains a small yellow star, representing the three major geographical divisions of the country: Luzon, Visayas, and Mindanao

National Sport: arnis, a form of martial arts

National Anthem: "Lupang Hinirang" ("Chosen Land")

National Tree: Narra

National Flower: sampaguita, waling-waling

National Bird: The Philippine eagle

Source: *CIA World Factbook*: Philippines
https://www.cia.gov/library/publications/the-world-factbook/geos/rp.html

In the city of Kalibo on Panay Island, the Ati-Atihan Festival is the year's biggest celebration. Participants honor the Ati tribe's millennia-old culture by wearing colorful costumes.

Early Arrivals

Nothing compares to the Ati-Atihan annual festival on the island of Panay during the third week of January. According to the *Lonely Planet* guidebook, "The elements of Ati-Atihan date back to the 13th century, when a group of lightskinned Malay immigrants from Borneo chose to show their regard for the local Ati people by painting their faces black and singing and dancing in thanks for the land and food that was offered to them (worried about any pagan origins, the colonizing Spanish later added Santo Niño [Baby Jesus] into the mix)."[1]

The festival lasts for several days. It begins at dawn each day and lasts long after midnight. Body painters compete in contests, while dancers in colorful costumes fill the streets. Part parade, part party, the Ati-Atihan is one of the biggest celebrations in the Philippines. It attracts hordes of locals and tourists, who book every room in local hotels.

The festival begins with a formal Catholic mass. On the second day, groups representing different tribes compete for attention and prizes. Soot-covered celebrants imitate the Atis (or Aetas), the original settlers of the Philippines. The festival name actually means "to be like the Atis."

Today, members of the Ati tribe can still be found in the backwoods of Panay and other islands. Thirty thousand years ago, the first Atis migrated from the modern-day countries of Indonesia, Malaysia, Singapore, and Thailand to the Philippines. Much of the world was frozen in an ice age, and even warmer climates felt its effects. Sea levels were lower. Areas that today are underwater were revealed, offering land bridges from the Malay Peninsula and the island of Borneo to the Philippine Islands.

Tens of thousands of years ago, people did not farm. They did not raise animals. They survived by hunting and gathering, stalking prey, and eating whatever they could find. It was an unpredictable way of life. When food supplies grew scarce, they moved on. Over time, the Atis moved further inland, to the forests and the mountains which offered better food supplies.

They were particularly hard-hit by the eruption of Mount Pinatubo. Many Ati villages were buried beneath several feet of ash. The inhabitants were forced into government-sponsored tent cities. As Sister Balazo, a Catholic nun who spent years living with them, said, "They really think of Mount Pinatubo as the mother who nursed them, bringing them water, the green forest and the animals."[2] This faith helped to sustain them during the crisis and believe that things would get better. Farmer Ernesto Abijon—who is half Ati, half Filipino— noted that "I don't believe that this soil is destroyed forever. It is just covered by a layer of sand and it can be taken away. I plan to live here when the volcano will go normal. I want to plant and harvest here— camote [a root crop] and banana."[3]

By the time the land bridges disappeared—buried beneath the ocean or eroded by water—many inhabitants lived far from the coast. The second wave of settlers consisted largely of fishermen and farmers. Sometime around 3200 BCE, they rode on crude boats from China and the Malay Peninsula.

These people spoke an early Malay language. They were also the islands' first rice farmers. The crop thrived in shallow water, and it was grown both in lowland areas and on the islands' hillsides. Tending and harvesting the crop led to early settlements and small villages devoted to its production.

Around 1200 CE, large boats sailed from the island of Borneo. When they reached Panay, they formed a new community. Unlike earlier groups, the newcomers had a written language. Before then, the groups on the Philippines had an oral history. This means they told stories about how they came to the region and how the earliest people survived.

The arrivals from Borneo had written laws and used money to buy goods. They were more advanced than the people who had been living in the Philippines for centuries. Usually when more advanced civilizations encounter less advanced ones, the advanced civilization takes over. This did not happen.

Although the two groups may have fought in the beginning, the Atis and the new arrivals soon helped each other. This is the origin of the Ati-Atihan, which celebrates the cooperation between the newcomers and Panay's natives.

Despite getting along with the Atis, the groups that fled Borneo did not get along very well with each other. They often fought. On the mainland of Southeast Asia, small groups were taken over by larger ones. Eventually empires were formed. This did not happen in the Philippines. Instead the communities developing on the islands had limited contact with each other. Each small group developed its own languages and customs. Rather than developing complex forms of government, most natives kept their way of life quite simple. Power rested with a tribal leader or chief who made the decisions.

By the time settlers from Borneo reached Panay, other islanders were trading with China and the Middle East. Other than a few records of trade between China and the northernmost islands, there is little information available about the Philippines before the 1500s. Still, by 1000 CE, traders came to the Philippines with more than goods. They brought a new religion as well.

Established in the 14th century, the Sheik Karimal Makdum Mosque in the island province of Tawi-Tawi still holds its four original pillars within the newer building.

Muslim Encounters

Because it is closer to Malaysia than to the larger islands of the Philippines, Simunul Island would often go unnoticed were it not for the Sheik Karim al Makdum Mosque. The oldest mosque in the Philippines, it was named after the Arab trader who first built it out of logs and mud in 1380. A national treasure, the mosque today is a colorful display of green and white. The pillars from the original mosque rest inside. These pillars are a reminder of the beginnings of Islam in the Philippines. The first monotheistic religion in the Philippines, it would spread across the southern islands and reach all the way to Manila.

Today no matter what official religion Filipinos believe in, many of them are connected to a religion practiced thousands of years before Islam. Even in the 21st century, more than one-third of Filipinos still work on farms. Many of these rural Filipinos take comfort from this oldest belief system, which is known as animism. It is a religion that sees supernatural powers in nature—in rocks and caves, in the forests, and in the mountains.

Animists believe powerful spirits control whether a crop has enough rain or endures a drought, whether seasonal monsoons will be helpful or deadly, and if a seemingly placid mountain will erupt into a deadly volcano. Native tribes across the world, including the Americas, have practiced forms of this belief.

Filipinos still consult diwateros. These women claim to be able to tell what a spirit wants. In rural areas, Filipinos often carry an anting-

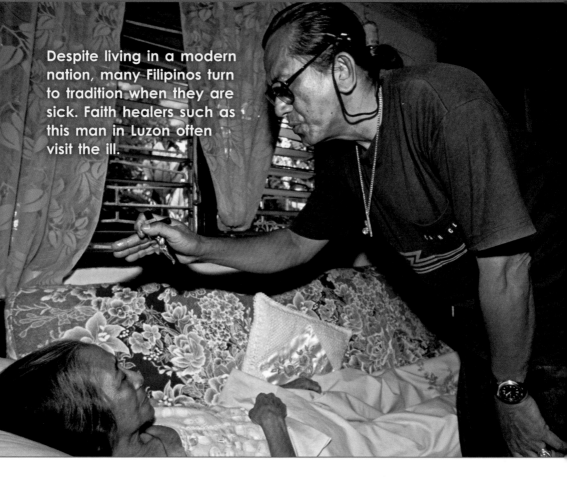

Despite living in a modern nation, many Filipinos turn to tradition when they are sick. Faith healers such as this man in Luzon often visit the ill.

anting, a good-luck charm worn around the neck to ward off evil and bring good luck. Many people go to faith healers. These men and women pray for a victim of illness to get better. Faith healers in the Philippines are often Christian, but the practice began thousands of years before Christ's birth.

Tribes living on the thousands of islands which became the Philippines freely worshiped as they wished for centuries. As outsiders began arriving, new religions were introduced.

Before 1000 CE, traders from China may have brought Buddhism to the Philippines. This religion began in India and taught that the key to happiness was ending all desire.

A few hundred years later, the first Muslim missionaries arrived. Although traders from the Middle East may have introduced Islam to the native tribes, these missionaries were the first group whose only goal was conversion.

Muslims believe the prophet Muhammad was visited by the angel Gabriel in 610 CE. This angel gave him verses from God which became Islam's holiest book, the Quran. Believers see Muhammad as the last in a line of holy men who included Moses and Jesus Christ.

Even before Muhammad's death, there would be violent conflicts between the religion he founded and older religions like Christianity and Judaism. Still, Islam reached the southern edge of the Philippines relatively peacefully. It was here, on Mindanao along with the Sulu Archipelago, that Islamic missionaries converted tribespeople.

Sulu was the home of the first centralized government, as it was led by a sultan in 1450. As a sultanate, the religion's influence spread across the Philippines. The sultan would keep control of the southern portion of the Philippines until the early 1900s. Even today parts of Mindanao and other islands in the south are closed to outsiders.

As Cesar Majul, a distinguished professor at the University of the Philippines, observes, "What gave the Muslims in the Philippines their cohesion and sense of community was Islam. It was Islam that institutionalized their loyalty to their Sultans, gave them a system of writing, sanctioned their attempts to resist alien rule, and gave a religious character to their patriotism."[1]

Natives who did not want to convert to Islam often fled to the mountains. Further north, many more would flee when the first Europeans arrived. Led by one of Portugal's most famous explorers, these Europeans didn't just want trade or conversion. They wanted control.

FYI FACT:

The Malay language was written in Arabic script called Jawi. After Arabic and Persian, Malay is the third most common form of Islamic writing.

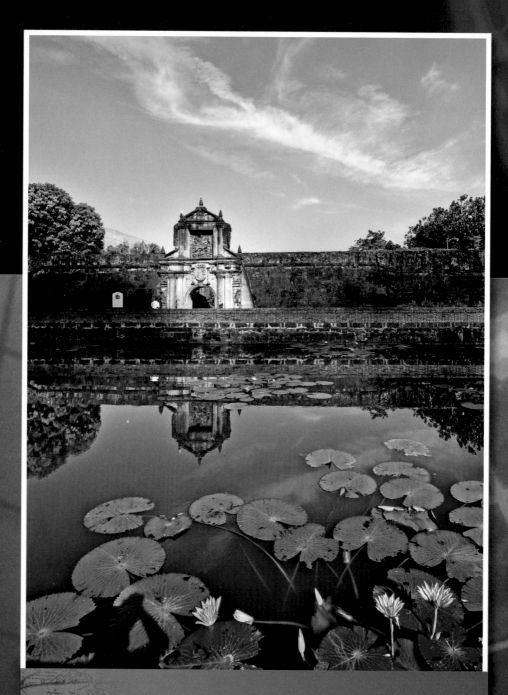

Enduring for more than 400 years, Fort Santiago is now a popular destination for visitors. Built by conquistador Miguel Lopez de Legazpi, it represented Spanish power over the locals.

The Spanish
Take Control

The ancient fort looms over the mouth of the Pasig River. Close to the cobblestone streets and shops of Intramuros, the oldest part of Manila, Fort Santiago is a popular draw for the city's visitors. Built more than 400 years ago, it remains as a monument to Spanish power. The fort's walls are scarred and worn but otherwise little changed from their completion in 1590.

Almost one thousand years ago, the inventions, silks, and spices of China were carried over a land route known as the Silk Road. The goods made their way to Venice, Italy, where local merchants sold them across Europe. Other European countries like the Netherlands, Portugal, and Spain began seeking a water route to Asia as an alternative to the Venetian dominance of trade from that region.

In the 1400s, Portuguese explorers sailed deep into the Atlantic Ocean. Expeditions sponsored by Portugal's Prince Henry the Navigator and his successors sailed along the coast of Africa and beyond. In 1498, Vasco da Gama rounded the tip of Africa and sailed all the way to India.

Five years earlier, Pope Alexander IV had divided New World discoveries between Spain and Portugal. On June 7, 1494, the Treaty of Tordesillas created an imaginary line between the Cape Verde Islands, controlled by Portugal, and Hispaniola, which Christopher Columbus had claimed for Spain. The treaty did more than ignore the claims of competing European powers. It ignored any people who lived on land the countries might claim.

Prince Henry the Navigator funded Portuguese explorations.

In 1529, the Treaty of Zaragoza did the same thing for the other side of the world. The Philippines lay within the area of Spanish control. Although Ferdinand Magellan was Portuguese and had even helped his country take control of Malacca in Malaysia, by 1517 he was ready to help Spain. Spanish King Charles V supported Magellan's quest to discover if ships could reach Asia by sailing west as well as east. Perhaps, the king hoped, there would be spice-producing islands within Spanish territory. Spices were especially important in this era. They helped preserve food, served as medicines, and disguised foul odors. The most sought-after spices were in Asian islands.

Setting sail with five ships on September 20, 1519, Magellan left Spain. He sailed down the east coast of South America, crossed the Pacific, and reached the Philippines on March 17, 1521. His two remaining ships anchored off the coast of Samar. Magellan claimed the land for Spain. He immediately set about converting the natives to Christianity.

Although Magellan succeeded in converting a number of locals, including several tribal chiefs, he made the mistake of backing one of those chiefs in an ongoing war. Magellan and 48 men went ashore to attack Lapu-Lapu, the opposing chief. Antonio Pigafetta, one of Magellan's men, described what happened next. "When we reached land, [the natives] had formed in three divisions to the number of more than one thousand five hundred people. When they saw us, they

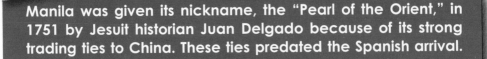

FYI FACT:

Manila was given its nickname, the "Pearl of the Orient," in 1751 by Jesuit historian Juan Delgado because of its strong trading ties to China. These ties predated the Spanish arrival.

charged down upon us with exceeding loud cries....They all hurled themselves upon him [Magellan]. One of them wounded him on the left leg with a large cutlass, which resembles a scimitar, only being larger. That caused the captain to fall face downward, when immediately they rushed upon him with iron and bamboo spears and with their cutlasses."[1] Today many Filipinos regard Lapu-Lapu as their first national hero because of his resistance to the Spanish invaders.

The death of Magellan barely slowed the Spanish conquest. In 1543, Ruy Lopez de Villalobos again claimed the island chain for Spain. He named it after the country's crown prince Felipe, calling it "Las Islas Filipinas."

The Spanish occupation of the region began in earnest 22 years later with the arrival of Miguel Lopez de Legazpi. Landing at Cebu, another island in the Visayan chain, he established a fort and a church. Legazpi had reached the Philippines from Mexico, where he had used harsh methods to control the natives opposing Spain. In the Philippines he used the same tactics, using his army to win battles against the Muslims. In 1571, he overcame a Muslim fort in an immense natural harbor on Luzon Island that he called Ciudad Insigne y Siempre Leal, which is Spanish for "Distinguished and Ever Loyal City." This lengthy name never caught on. Instead, people began calling it by the native word for mangrove: Maynilad. Today we know it as Manila.

Manila was the ideal harbor for the growing trade between China and Spain. Once a year, Chinese junks docked at Manila. They unloaded silks and other goods. Since the Chinese only accepted silver as payment, galleons loaded with silver from Spanish-controlled mines in Central and South America sailed from Acapulco, Mexico. The Philippines would be used primarily as a port until the 1800s. Only then would the Spanish begin exploiting its natural resources, exporting minerals such as gold, silver, and tin along with coffee and tobacco and exotic fruits like mangoes, pineapples and bananas.

Exploration was about more than discovering new trade routes and claiming land. The Catholic Church saw part of its mission as encouraging explorers to go into areas unvisited by Europeans and convert the locals to Christianity.

During Spanish rule, Catholic churches such as San Agustin were constructed across much of the Philippines. Today San Agustin is a World Heritage Site.

Today the sunny, peach-colored exterior of Manila's San Agustin Church reflects the bright palettes of the tropics. The gray stone monastery and convent, along with its lofty interiors, seem to reflect the power of the Catholic Church. Built in 1571, San Agustin is the oldest stone church in the Philippines. The church's founders arrived with Legazpi. Like other churches in the Philippines, San Agustin was self-supporting. Spain provided the churches with land, which they used for growing crops. Priests were the natives' primary source of education for several centuries as Catholic leaders built and ran schools across the Philippines. They also established hospitals.

There was yet another legacy. As authors Alfredo Roces and Grace Roces explain, "To Christianize Filipinos, Spanish missionaries drew them into population centers. A program of putting potential converts 'under church bells' (bajo las campanas) was vigorously pursued, thus leading to the formation of towns with the church as their center, the populace within hearing distance of its bells. The bigger the bells, the larger the community."[2]

No other country in Southeast Asia was dominated by a colonizer's religion like the Philippines. More than 400 years after the first priest arrived, today over 90% of Filipinos are Christian. The vast majority are Catholic. Despite native anger toward Spain, the locals held onto their new faith. Once Fort Santiago and other forts were completed, Muslim influence in the central and northern islands disappeared. Islam remained strong across the southern portion of the Philippines; no matter how powerful the Spanish became, they could not take over this region.

A few natives resisted both the Christian and the Muslim missionaries, fleeing the low-lying coastal areas for remote mountains.

FYI FACT:

In 1912, U.S. army officer Cornélis De Witt Willcox wrote a book about the Ilongots (also known as Bugkalots). Although the tribe only numbered a few thousand, they controlled a large and hard-to-reach region of Luzon's jungles and mountains. Willcox wrote that they attacked the town of Dúpax, killing people and taking their heads. Today the tribe no longer practices headhunting.

The central portions of larger islands like Luzon remained unexplored until the 1800s. Here tribes maintained a way of life untouched by outside influences. The reputation of some of those tribes as headhunters was so frightening that most outsiders avoided the regions they controlled.

The Spanish altered the lives of the island's natives, calling them "Indios." They were not considered the equal of the Spanish who took their land, then forced them to work on it for very low wages. The Spanish even taxed the money the natives earned working on land they had once owned!

The way the Spanish treated the natives unified the tribes. Before their arrival, they had little contact with each other. Each tribe viewed itself as unique. The Spanish gave the natives their first sense of belonging to a country. By creating the Philippines, the Spanish inspired natives to see themselves as Filipinos.

Because it was so valuable, the Philippines was highly sought after. Over the next three centuries, Spain fought with the Chinese, the Japanese, the Dutch, and the English, along with Muslims, for control of the islands. Spain won all of these battles. Yet the hardest battles would not be fought against fellow colonizers but against natives who dreamed of freedom. By the late 1800s, natives looked to the example of the United States—a place where people could vote and where an ideal of limited government gave the poor opportunities to become rich. Yet for many Filipinos the U.S. would become yet another occupier rather than a symbol of freedom.

During the Battle of Manila Bay on May 1, 1898, the USS *Olympia* helped destroy the Spanish fleet. Ten Spanish warships were sunk or captured at the cost of six wounded American sailors.

The U.S. Moves in

The battleship USS *Maine* had been anchored in the harbor of Havana, Cuba for several weeks in early 1898. On the night of February 15th, an explosion ripped through the ship. Most of the sailors were asleep. The blast destroyed most of the ship's forward third. Two-hundred-sixty-six men died in the disaster. Afterward, several investigations were unable to discover the reason for the explosion.

Across the United States, newspapers and their readers blamed Spain—which had controlled Cuba since the early 1500s—for the catastrophe. In the Philippines, Spanish control had been steadily weakening. For over a century, natives had been fighting against the colonizers. Although it occurred nearly halfway around the world, the explosion of the *Maine* would soon provide the catalyst for their overthrow.

Southeast Asia's nationalist movement was born in the Philippines. A movement driven by a desire for independence and their own nation, it was sometimes strengthened by Spanish influence.

Foreign trade helped elite Filipinos grow wealthy. They were able to send their children overseas to be educated at the best schools. When they returned, they brought new ideas about government and their country's future. Despite their education, most had few opportunities besides assisting the Spanish. Filipino priests were unable to join religious orders controlled by the Spanish. In 1872, three native priests were executed for preaching against Spanish control. Educated Filipinos looked to the United States as a model. After all, the U.S. had been a colony of England until declaring independence in 1776.

In the last decade of the 19th century, the independence movement gained strength. An office clerk named Andres Bonifacio helped to form Katipuan (Sons of the People), one of the main organizations promoting Filipino independence. A rivalry developed between Bonifacio and a local chief, Emilio Aguinaldo, who was opposed to violence. He wanted to see Katipuan inspire political reforms and viewed the U.S. system as ideal. Despite Aguinaldo's opposition to violence, after his supporters elected him president of the organization they executed Bonifacio.

Spanish leaders were worried. Aguinaldo was promised reforms if he left the country. He agreed, relocating to Hong Kong along with a number of his supporters.

The reforms never happened. Meanwhile, another champion of independence had matched Aguinaldo's fame. Jose Rizal was a doctor and scientist who wrote novels challenging Spanish rule and promoting nationalism. Because his work was seen as a serious threat to Spanish control, in 1896 he was executed by a firing squad. The execution only served to further inflame Filipino anger. His legacy continues to this day. "No self-respecting town in the country is without a statue of the man, or does not have a major street named after him," notes guidebook author Ralph Jennings. "Reverence for thinker Dr. Jose Rizal, who died a martyr at age 35 in the last years of Spanish rule,

FYI FACT:

In 1744, Francisco Dagohoy led a revolt against the Spanish on the island of Bohol. Driven by their anger over forced labor and high taxes, the rebels seized control of the island's mountains and caves. The revolt eventually boasted 20,000 Filipino followers and outlasted 20 different Spanish governor-generals. It lasted until 1829, when Spanish authorities used native soldiers and heavy artillery to crush the resistance.

Larap

has spanned a century and spread to foreign lands."[1]

As was the case in the Philippines, Cuban revolutionaries were attacking Spanish control of their island. The *Maine* had been sent to Havana to protect U.S citizens as violence increased. The U.S. declared war on Spain on April 25, 1898, just over two months after the explosion.

On May 1, Commodore George Dewey led a U.S. fleet into Manila Bay against an overmatched Spanish fleet. The Spanish ships were destroyed without the combat loss of a single American life. That month, Aguinaldo returned to the Philippines. This

Emilio Aguinaldo led fellow Filipinos against the U.S. occupation.

time he had the U.S. as an ally in his fight against Spain.

On June 12, 1898, Aguinaldo declared the Philippines' independence. In August, the war ended. Another one was right around the corner.

For $20 million dollars, the U.S. bought the Philippines from Spain while also gaining control of Puerto Rico, Guam, and Cuba's Guantanamo Bay. Although the U.S. promised the Filipinos they would gain independence, Aguinaldo and his supporters worried that it was just one more lie from a powerful country. Now in control of the Philippine Army, he launched an attack against U.S. forces in Manila on February 4, 1899.

The U.S. victory over Spain had been quick and decisive. This new war against the Philippines dragged on for over three years. More than 4,000 Americans and 20,000 Filipinos died in the conflict. Aguinaldo was finally captured by U.S. forces in March of 1901 and swore an oath of allegiance to the U.S. The war ended soon afterward.

At one point, Aguinaldo was so discouraged that he said his soldiers had died without making any difference on future events. That opinion may not have been entirely correct. The U.S. quickly set a long-term timeline for Philippine independence, with an official date set for 1944. In the meantime, the country's elite officials and landowners gave their support to the Americans. Under civilian governor (and future U.S. president) William Howard Taft, steps were undertaken to prepare Filipinos for self-rule. Compulsory education was instituted, requiring the young to attend school, and a national health program began.

By 1935, the Philippines had a constitution based on the U.S. Constitution when Manuel L. Quezon became the first president elected by the commonwealth government. Dreams of independence, however, would soon be delayed.

On November 26, 1941, six of Japan's front-line aircraft carriers headed to sea. Their destination was the U.S. naval base at Pearl Harbor, Hawaii. The carriers were accompanied by fast battleships, cruisers and destroyers, along with tankers for refueling during the Pacific crossing.

Just before 8:00 AM on December 7th, the first attack wave struck. A second wave followed soon after. Before the morning was out, five of the eight U.S. battleships in the harbor were sinking or sunk, most American combat planes were smoking ruins, and over 2,400 Americans were killed. The United States responded by declaring war, joining the conflict which would be known as World War II. The day after the attack, the Japanese bombed Singapore and landed troops on southern Thailand and northern Malaya.

The Japanese also had their eyes on the Philippines. Survivors were still being fished out of the water at Pearl Harbor when it was the islands' turn to face the Japanese onslaught.

The Spanish-American War was perhaps the swiftest in U.S. history, lasting for less than four months. Here American troops relax on a bridge over the Pasig River in Manila on August 12, 1898, the day when the conflict officially ended.

U.S. forces were spread thin and unprepared when Japanese forces attacked the Philippines. In May of 1942, American troops waved the white flag of surrender at Corregidor Island after enduring weeks of nearly constant shelling and bombing. Nearly 11,000 were taken prisoner.

Aftermath

The Japanese attack on the Philippines began with bombing air bases near Manila, virtually wiping out American air power. Two weeks later, more than 40,000 Japanese troops swarmed ashore on Luzon. They easily pushed American and Filipino forces into the Bataan Peninsula, located at the western edge of Manila Bay. For almost three months, the defenders gradually gave ground to the much better-equipped Japanese troops. Food and ammunition supplies dwindled. Disease was rampant.

After surrendering in April 1942, over 10,000 Americans and 60,000 Filipinos were forced to march more than 60 miles under blazing sunlight to a prison camp. They were given very little food and water. Many died from the heat and dehydration. Others were executed by Japanese soldiers. By the time they arrived at the prisoner of war camp, more than 7,000 had died. This atrocity became infamous as the "Bataan Death March." The following month, the final American garrison on Corregidor Island fell to the invaders.

The commander of the U.S. and Philippine forces, General Douglas MacArthur, had evacuated the islands under the orders of President Franklin D. Roosevelt. He promised to return. It would be well over two horrific years before he could keep his promise.

Conditions were scarcely better for those left behind. Although many Filipino political leaders helped the invaders, most people in the Philippines viewed these leaders as puppets, controlled by the Japanese. The new occupiers treated Filipinos worse than the Spanish colonizers.

In 1942, General Douglas MacArthur left the Philippines in defeat. He promised to return. In October of 1944, he waded ashore at Leyte Island.

They forced many people to work long hours and abused those who didn't. The country's growing Chinese population was singled out for especially brutal treatment. Many of them were tortured, or even killed.

Although the Japanese declared the country "independent," this term meant almost nothing. Japanese interests overwhelmed any potential freedoms. In response to their harsh treatment, some Filipinos—often under the command of American soldiers who had fled into the jungles instead of surrendering—conducted guerrilla warfare on the occupiers.

The United States had entered World War II following an early morning attack. They ended the war the same way. In August of 1945, U.S. planes dropped atomic bombs on the Japanese cities of Nagasaki and Hiroshima. Japan surrendered.

Honoring a pledge made decades earlier, the U.S. granted Philippine independence and self-rule on July 4, 1946. General MacArthur said that America had buried imperialism on that day. The Philippines was the first constitutional democracy in Asia and one of the first colonies after World War II to win self-rule. Most colonies did not become independent until years later.

For Filipinos, the years following independence were filled with challenges. With so many leaders suspected of aiding the Japanese occupiers, General MacArthur reassured voters that longtime politician

Manuel Roxas was not one of them. In 1946, Roxas was elected
president of the Philippines.

The United States provided millions of dollars in economic aid and
maintained two important military bases in the Philippines: Clark Air
Base and U.S. Naval Base Subic Bay. American companies also enjoyed
trade protections.

Yet for poor Filipinos, life was little changed from before the war.
Landowners still held the country's political power and wealth. There
were few opportunities or privileges for the men and women who
worked on the land.

Divisions between those with money and those without helped fuel
a communist uprising. In 1948, the Hukbalahaps—primarily peasant
farmers living in central Luzon—began fighting Filipino military forces.

They used violence, trying to
convince Filipino leaders to
divide the country's large estates
among poor farmers. Worried
about a communist takeover, the
United States provided military
support to the government.

Philippines secretary of
defense Ramon Magsaysay
began a series of reforms to help
the poor in the 1950s. These
reforms, along with U.S. military
support, ended the Hukbalahap
rebellion in 1954. Magsaysay
had been elected president the
previous year.

**The flag of the Philippines is
raised while the U.S. flag is
lowered during ceremonies
on July 4, 1946 which
granted full independence
to the new nation.**

During Magsaysay's presidency, he instituted pro-growth policies which improved the average Filipino's standard of living by attracting businesses. Taking advantage of the prosperity that followed the end of World War II, many people in the U.S. and across the world began buying everything from cars to television sets. Countries that had factories with inexpensive workers or essential raw materials benefited from this increased buying. The Philippines offered both.

By 1957, the Philippines' rate of growth was second only to Japan among Asian countries. The horrors of war and the economic turmoil which followed were receding. Then tragedy struck. On March 17, Magsaysay's plane crashed in Cebu.

Vice President Carlos P. Garcia served until 1961 when his vice president, Diosdado Macapagal, was elected president. In 1965, Ferdinand Marcos won the presidency. Even though the constitution limited him to serving two four-year terms, Marcos ruled for more than 20 years. He used the power of the presidency to enrich himself and his friends. His wife, Imelda, was a former beauty queen who became well-known for her wealthy lifestyle. She was especially noted for her vast collection of shoes, many of which were worth hundreds of dollars a pair.

Even as Marcos grew rich, the country grew poorer. Its place as an economic power slipped. Despite growing opposition to his presidency, the United States continued providing economic and military support. U.S. leaders were more concerned about a communist resurgence than Marcos's brutal leadership.

In 1969, Marcos was reelected. During his second term, Muslims in the southern islands demanded independence. Marcos sent his army into the region to put down numerous uprisings across Mindanao. At

FYI FACT:

Today, Filipinos don't do much celebrating on July 4th. Instead, most Filipinos celebrate Independence Day on June 12th. This honors the day in 1898 when the country declared its independence from Spain.

With the support of the Philippine military and the United States, Ferdinand Marcos and his wife Imelda behaved more like king and queen than freely elected leaders. Here they visit Mobile, Alabama in 1982.

the same time, communists had reorganized as the New People's Army. They began attacking military installations and fought with the army in the jungles of Luzon.

In 1972, Marcos declared a national emergency and put the country under martial law. He abolished Congress while suspending a newly written constitution. He restricted labor parties and political groups which opposed him while taking control of the media. He would be president until the "crisis" ended. It lasted over a decade.

During the 1970s, the price of oil—an important Philippine import—increased. Many of the country's exports, however, commanded a lower price. The combination of economic and political uncertainty created unrest. Some people publicly protested his presidency while others wrote about the country's problems.

By the 1980s, the Philippines was being called "the sick man of Asia." The country was drowning in debt, money lent to it by other governments which included the United States. By then, hundreds of

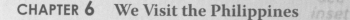

Benigno Aquino, Jr. was a political rival of Marcos, and a champion of the Filipino people. Returning home from surgery, he was assassinated at the Manila Airport. The body of his alleged killer, Rolando Galman, lies on the tarmac in the lower left corner as security forces lift Aquino into a van.

Marcos's opponents had been imprisoned and even killed. Yet despite the dangers, two men consistently spoke out against him.

Manila's Cardinal Jaime Sin was the Catholic Church's leader in the Philippines. Most members of his congregation were poor. He spoke about how hard their lives were under the Marcos regime and pushed for change.

While Sin spoke for the country's Catholic majority, Benigno Aquino Jr. represented hope for voters. Elected as a senator in 1967, many expected that Aquino would become president after Marcos served two terms in 1973. Instead, Marcos extended his presidency. He also accused Aquino of supporting the rebels in Luzon.

Aquino was imprisoned for seven years on murder charges, but was allowed to travel to the U.S. for heart surgery in 1980. Three years later, he returned to the Philippines. Aquino was leaving his plane at the Manila Airport when shots rang out. Marcos's most powerful opponent crumpled to the ground. His killer, Rolando Galman, was shot to death. Although Marcos was blamed for the assassination, it was never proven.

Images of Aquino's bullet-riddled body led TV newscasts and gained front-page coverage of newspapers across the world. Aquino was seen as a martyr who had died in the cause of his people's freedom. In the Philippines, supporters flooded the streets protesting Marcos and accusing him of responsibility for Aquino's death.

Marcos held onto power for two more years. During this time, Cardinal Sin comforted Aquino's grieving widow, Corazon. He motivated her to make what some considered a reckless choice. She ran for the presidency of the Philippines. Right from the start, she encountered a significant problem. The Marcos-controlled media refused to give her equal access. "Cardinal Sin's regular radio addresses on the Catholic radio station calling for the people to support her became a critical tool to rally millions to her side," the *New York Times* reported. "He became known in Manila as the 'unseen general' who handed down on earth orders from above."[1]

The 1986 election was riddled with fraud, voter intimidation, and violence. Although Aquino won the popular vote, Marcos's supporters in the National Assembly voted that he should remain president. In the streets of Manila and across the country, Aquino supporters joined with Catholics to protest. Corazon Aquino did all she could to keep the protests peaceful.

The protests reached a peak in late February. Hundreds of Aquino supporters marched down Edsa, a major Manila street. Their path was blocked by the Philippine Army, armed with guns and tanks. The protestors were armed only with signs and flowers. Bloodshed seemed inevitable.

Benigno Aquino, Jr.'s widow, Corazon, was a political novice who took up the cause of her murdered husband. Seen here on December 8, 1989, she is guarded by security men as she addresses a rally of 40,000 supporters in Manila. Her hand gestures stand for "L" (Laban, or "fight").

Facing off against the Philippine army, the front lines of what was known as the People Power Revolution were made up of priests and nuns. They kneeled before the soldiers and began to pray. For a moment, nothing happened. And then the army controlled by Ferdinand Marcos stood down. The people had won.

Corazon Aquino—affectionately known as Cory—was sworn in as president on February 25, 1986. Ferdinand Marcos and his wife Imelda fled the country. He died three years later in Hawaii. Imelda eventually returned to the Philippines, where she was elected to the House of Representatives several times. According to some estimates, her family may have amassed a fortune of $10 billion, much of it money given from the U.S. to help the Philippine people.

The year after Aquino became president, a new constitution was implemented. It was the country's fifth since 1898. The new constitution limited the president to a single six-year term. The vice president could serve two. The constitution also provided for freedom of speech and of religion and the right to a fair trial.

Despite the excitement of the election, the Aquino administration faced numerous challenges. There was a major earthquake and a volcanic eruption. There were half a dozen attempts to overthrow her. Yet during her term, the country's rate of growth climbed. She helped attract more foreign investment and privatized many businesses that had been controlled by Marcos and his friends in the government. As *Philippine Star* columnist Elfren S. Cruz noted when she died, "For

Despite economic and political progress, the Philippines was challenged by the nation's Muslim minority. Separatist movements like the Moro Islamic Liberation Front battled Philippine troops, seen here on January 28, 2007 in Rangaban Village on Mindanao.

17 years after her presidency, Cory was not just a former president. She was the moral conscience of the Filipino people. She was the only person who could call the people to the streets to express public outrage against the machinations and corruption of even the highest and most powerful politicians."[1]

Her successor, Fidel Ramos, oversaw increased growth as well when he lowered tax rates and sold large government-run industries like banking and oil to private companies. Although the Philippines suffered during an economic crisis in 1998 and another in 2008, overall it recovered faster than many other countries in the region.

The election of former movie star Joseph Estrada in 1998 was a setback for the country. In many ways, he governed as Marcos had—giving prime jobs to his friends and stealing from the government. In 2001 he was removed from office.

Estrada's vice president, Gloria Macapagal-Arroyo, became president. In 2004, she won election to the office. Although the economy improved, the country faced numerous challenges. Muslim Moros in the south continued fighting against the Philippine government. Today the U.S. embassy advises travelers to avoid this region because of its dangers.

The Philippines remains one of the poorest countries in Asia. Many of its citizens remain out of work, while the poor in the cities often live in rundown government housing or crudely built shacks.

FYI FACT:

Francis Ford Coppola's movie *Apocalypse Now* was filmed in the Philippines in 1979. The production was slowed down by typhoons and star Martin Sheen's heart attack. It went over budget by nearly $20 million and took four times as long to make as originally planned.

Although the most popular forms of music in the Philippines are karaoke (where everyday people sing live before an audience to a recorded track) and cover bands, Filipino Arnel Pineda became famous when he was selected as the lead singer of the U.S. group Journey in 2007. In 2009, he performed with the band during the pregame show at the Super Bowl.

Still, more than 90% of Filipinos can read or write—far more than in many other poor countries. One quarter of all Filipinos attend college, such as the privately run University of the East in Manila. The country is investing in education and high tech in hopes of attracting more foreign business.

The country has a growing arts scene as well. Beginning after World War II, numerous low-budget movies have been made in the Philippines. American movie producers often use the jungle as a setting and

Late in the day on November 7, 2013, what would be called "Super Typhoon Haiyan" slammed into the Philippines. Sustained winds exceeded 160 miles per hour (260 kilometers per hour), with estimates of gusts up to 235 miles per hour (380 kilometers per hour). Tacloban on Leyte Island (seen here) was among the hardest hit areas, with the first reported casualties. Over 5,000 people lost their lives in the disaster.

sometimes involve the country's army in stunts with gunfights and helicopters. Although the country's mainstream movie studios have declined since the 1990s, independent films from the Filipinos have won awards and worldwide audiences. And there are signs that the industry may be undergoing a revival. Yam Laranas, a noted Filipino director, says that "There has been a revolution in technology. Ten years ago, few people could afford to make an independent film in the Philippines. A nontraditional story was not economically viable. Things are changing. A lot of independent directors and studios are making innovative films because the costs are so much lower. It is less of a risk."[2]

In 2010, Benigno "Noynoy" Aquino III, the son of Benigno and Corazon Aquino, was elected president. In 2012 he signed a peace agreement with the Moros, hoping to end further bloodshed in the area. The economy grew by over six percent, while private investment grew. Many remain hopeful that he will fulfill the promise of his parents.

This monument honors Josefa Llanes Escoda, founder of the Girl Scouts of the Philippines. Escoda helped many prisoners of war during World War II. Sadly, she was executed by the Japanese.

Chapter 8

Filipinos to Know

The Philippines has many talented and famous people, including writers, activists and politicians. Here are a few of them.

Fernando Amorsolo (1892–1972)
Amorsolo was apprenticed when he was 13 to his mother's first cousin, Fabian de la Rosa (1869–1937), a popular Filipino artist who produced over 1,000 works during his lifetime. Amorsolo became even more famous, with paintings that included colorful landscapes, atmospheric effects, and figures. He is especially known for his use of backlighting and willingness to take risks. He is also highly regarded for his depictions of women. "Women are painted like no other did,"[1] said a curator from the Ayala Museum, which is located in Metro Manila. He painted portraits of General Douglas MacArthur, and scenes of war like "Bataan." His "Afternoon Meal of the Workers" won first prize at the New York World's Fair in 1939. In 2008, seven museums and galleries honored him with extensive exhibitions of his work.

Corazon "Cory" Aquino (1933–2009)
After receiving her college education at the College of Mount Saint Vincent in New York City, Aquino returned to the Philippines and married Benigno S. Aquino Jr. Her husband had a quick rise in politics, becoming a governor and then a senator. Aquino became a housewife and often hosted parties for her husband's political followers. Benigno opposed then-president Ferdinand Marcos. He was arrested and then

sent into exile in the United States, accompanied by his family. When he was assassinated upon his return in 1983, his widow assumed his leadership role even though she had no formal political background. In 1986, she ran for president against Marcos. "When she went to fill out her application for the presidency, Corazon Aquino had nothing to enter under OCCUPATION but 'Housewife,'" according to *Time* magazine. "The last office for which the soft-spoken widow had been chosen was valedictorian of her sixth-grade class. In fact, her chief, if not her only, political strengths seemed to be her innocence of politics and the moral symbolism of her name."[2] In spite of widespread fraud, she won the election. She was the first female president of an Asian nation. She instituted numerous reforms and moved the country far from the harsh control of the Marcos regime. Many people regard her as "the mother of Philippine democracy" and *Time* magazine named her "Person of the Year" in 1986. She died of colon cancer in 2009.

Josefa Llanes Escoda (1898–1945)
Escoda worked as a teacher and social worker with the American Red Cross, and was active in the movement to give Filipino women the right to vote. In the 1930s she organized the Girl Scouts of the Philippines and became the organization's first executive director. Unfortunately, things were about to change. "At the height of Japanese occupation in the Philippines during the Second World War, Josefa and her husband selflessly and tirelessly helped many Filipino and American prisoners in several concentration camps," says Philippines guidebook author Harry Ballais. "Thus, Escoda was hailed as the Florence Nightingale of the Philippines."[3] She and her husband were imprisoned by the Japanese for their resistance to the occupation. Both were executed by their captors. She appears on the 1,000-peso bill as one of three Filipinos martyred by the Japanese.

Ramon Magsaysay (1907–1957)
Widely considered one of the best presidents in Philippine history, Magsaysay worked hard for political and economic reforms to help the poor. An automobile mechanic, he became an important guerrilla

Ramon Magsaysay helped the Philippines become a modern nation. His economic and political reforms raised the country's standard of living, but his efforts ended abruptly with his tragic death in a plane crash.

leader on Luzon during World War II. Encouraged to run for the House of Representatives by his wartime comrades, he was elected in 1946. Four years later, President Elpidio Quirino appointed him Secretary of National Defense. He used his own guerrilla experiences to defeat the Hukbalahap insurgency. Feeling that Quirino's administration was corrupt, he ran for president in 1953 and won decisively. He worked for agrarian reform and other policies to help his countrymen. His presidency was cut short when he died in a plane crash in March, 1957. An estimated five million people attended his burial. Shortly after his death, the Ramon Magsaysay Award was created. "The Ramon Magsaysay Award is given to persons—regardless of race, nationality, creed or gender—who address issues of human development in Asia with courage and creativity, and in doing so have made contributions which have transformed their societies for the better," notes the Award's website. "Collectively, the Awardees' stories paint a portrait of remarkable change and achievement in areas as diverse as rural and urban development, poverty alleviation, public health, the environment, governance, education, business, human rights, culture, and the arts."[4]

Manny Pacquiao (1978–)
Few—if any—Filipinos can boast a more diverse set of accomplishments than Manny Pacquiao, who emerged from a background of poverty to achieve worldwide fame. He is best-known for his accomplishments as a boxer. He has held major titles at weights ranging from 112 pounds to 154 pounds (51 kilograms to 70 kilograms). For years, he was regarded as the world's best boxer on a pound-for-pound basis. He has starred in movies. He has a fashion line and a popular brand of cologne. He was the first Filipino athlete to have a postage stamp in his honor. In 2007 he ran for the Philippine House of Representatives. Though he was defeated, he ran again three years later and easily won election. In 2013, no one ran against him and he was re-elected. By then, *Time* magazine had recognized him as one of the world's 100 most influential people. Former heavyweight boxer Lennox Lewis noted that "Manny has connected with the people of his home country, the Philippines, to the point where he's almost like a god. The people have rallied behind him and feel like they're a part of him, because they can see his talent, his dedication, his grace and his class. The grip he holds over the Philippines is similar to Nelson Mandela's influence in South Africa."[5]

Manny Pacquiao (on the right) is a national hero in the
Philippines, both as a politician and as a boxer. Here he defends
his world welterweight title against Juan Manuel Marquez of
Mexico. Pacquiao narrowly won the 12-round bout, which took
place at the MGM Grand Garden Arena in Las Vegas, Nevada,
on November 12, 2011.

Mamon

(Sponge Cake)

Mamon is the Filipino version of sponge cakes, which are soft and tasty. They are usually served as snacks, and can be topped with butter and grated cheddar cheese.

Ingredients:
2-½ cups all-purpose flour
1-½ cup white sugar
1 tablespoon baking powder
1 teaspoon salt
½ cup vegetable oil
8 egg yolks
2 tablespoons grated orange peel
1 teaspoon vanilla extract
⅓ cup orange juice
½ cup water
8 egg whites
½ teaspoon cream of tartar

Instructions:
Prepare the following recipe with adult supervision:
1. Preheat oven to 325°F (165°C). Grease 16 muffin cups.
2. Stir the flour, 1 cup of sugar, baking powder, and salt together in a large bowl.
3. Make a hole in the center of the flour mixture and add the oil, egg yolks, grated orange peel, vanilla extract, orange juice, and water. Mix well by hand until smooth.
4. Beat the egg whites with the cream of tartar until foamy in a glass or metal mixing bowl. Gradually add ½ cup sugar, continuing to beat until soft peaks form. Lift your beater or whisk straight up: the egg whites will form soft mounds rather than a sharp peak.
5. Fold the flour mixture into the egg whites.
6. Pour the resulting batter into the prepared muffin cups to about two-thirds full.
7. Bake until a toothpick inserted into the center comes out clean, about 40 minutes. Cool in the pans for 10 minutes before removing to cool completely on a wire rack.

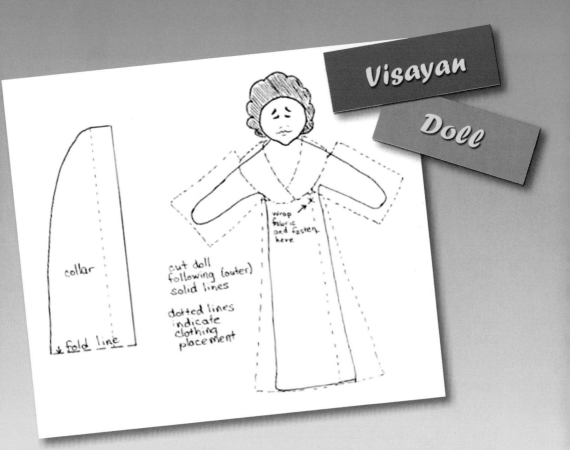

Visayan Doll

Inside the diagram:
- collar
- fold line
- cut doll following (outer) solid lines
- dotted lines indicate clothing placement
- wrap fabric and fasten here

If you lived in the Philippines, you would use natural fibers, such as the ones from the abaca tree, to make this doll. Instead, you can make it with common supermarket products such as cardboard, colorful printed paper, and paper napkins.

Materials
- Poster board or cardboard
- Paper napkins (with print)
- Striped paper, or paper with stripes painted or colored on
- Black felt-tip pen

Instructions
1. Draw and cut out the basic figure of the doll.
2. Color hair and draw face.
3. Cut collar pieces from napkin, using pattern shown.
4. Cut rectangles from the napkins for sleeves, and fold in half over the figure's arms.
5. Wrap striped fabric around as a skirt.

1521	Portuguese explorer Ferdinand Magellan arrives in the Philippines and is slain by native chieftain Lapu-Lapu in battle.
1543	A Spanish expedition under the command of Ruy Lopez de Villalobos claims the islands and names them the Philippines in honor of Felipe, the heir to the Spanish throne.
1565	An expedition led by Miguel Lopez de Legazpi establishes a Spanish settlement in Cebu.
1571	Spain takes control of the non-Islamic parts of the islands and monopolizes trade.
1821	The Philippines is governed directly from Spain rather than from New Spain in Mexico City.
1890s	An insurrection against Spanish rule begins.
1898	Following the U.S. victory in the Battle of Manila Bay, Spain sells the Philippines to the U.S. for $20 million under the terms of the Treaty of Paris.
1899	Insurgent activity begins against the U.S.
1900	The U.S. enacts a law that will grant the Philippines independence by 1944.
1902	Civilian government replaces military rule.
1935	Manuel L. Quezon is elected president and a new constitution is adopted, promising independence within 10 years.
1941	Japan invades the Philippines.
1945	U.S. military forces retake the islands.
1946	The U.S. grants independence to the Republic of the Philippines.
1951	Japan and the Philippines sign a peace treaty.
1965	Ferdinand Marcos becomes president.
1967	The Philippines joins the Association of Southeast Asian Nations (ASEAN).
1969	Marcos is re-elected.
1972	Marcos declares martial law.
1973	A new constitution is formed, giving Marcos absolute power.
1981	Martial law is lifted and Marcos wins re-election.
1983	Upon returning to the Philippines from exile in the United States, Senator Benigno S. Aquino Jr. is assassinated at the Manila airport.
1986	Corazon Aquino opposes Marcos in new elections and is declared the winner; Marcos is exiled to Hawaii.
1990	An earthquake kills over 1,600 people and causes hundreds of millions in damage.
1991	Mount Pinatubo erupts, causing extensive damage.
1998	Joseph Estrada is elected President.
2001	Estrada steps down and Gloria Arroyo becomes president.
2010	Benigno "Noynoy" Aquino III, the son of Benigno and Corazon Aquino, is elected president.
2014	The Philippine government and the country's largest Muslim rebel group reached accord in late January.

Chapter 1. The Philippines Overview
1. Edu Jarque, "Panagbenga Festival 2013: Seeing stars among the flowers." *The Philippine Star,* March 7, 2013. http://www.philstar.com/entertainment/2013/03/07/916672/panagbenga-festival-2013-seeing-stars-among-flowers
2. "Mt. Pinatubo's cloud shades global climate," *Science News*, July 18, 1992. http://www.thefreelibrary.com/Mt.+Pinatubo%27s+cloud+shades+global+climate.-a012467057

Chapter 2. Early Arrivals
1. "Ati-Atigan: a guide to the Philippines' exultant 800 year old festival." LonelyPlanet.com: "Philippines," July 27, 2012. http://www.lonelyplanet.com/philippines/travel-tips-and-articles/76270
2. Vernon Loeb, "Natives Who Worship Pinatubo Feel Its Wrath." *Seattle Times*, July 21, 1991. http://community.seattletimes.nwsource.com/archive/?date=19910721&slug=1295627
3. Ibid.

Chapter 3. Muslim Encounters
1. Wadja Esmula and Muhiddin Batara Mutia, "Islam in the Philippines." Islam and Muslims in the Philippines. http://www.islamawareness.net/Asia/Philippines/philippines.html

Chapter 4. The Spanish Take Control
1. "The Battle of Mactan. Lapu Lapu Versus Magellan." Mactan.com. http://lapulapu.weebly.com
2. Alfredo Roces and Grace Roces, *Culture Shock: Philippines* (Portland, Oregon: Graphic Arts Center Publishing Company, 2001), p. 144.

Chapter 5. The U.S. Moves In
1. Ralph Jennings, *Insight Guides: Philippines* (London: Insight Guides, 2013), p. 41.

Chapter 6. Aftermath
1. Michelle O'Donnell, "Cardinal Jaime Sin, a Champion of the Poor in the Philippines, Is Dead at 76." *New York Times*, June 21, 2005. http://www.nytimes.com/2005/06/21/obituaries/21sin.html

Chapter 7. The Philippines Today
1. Elfren S. Cruz, "Cory's legacy of leadership." *Philippine Star*, August 1, 2013. http://www.philstar.com/opinion/2013/08/01/1037511/corys-legacy-leadership
2. Floyd Whaley, "New Ambitions in Philippine Film Business." *New York Times*, May 7, 2012.http://www.nytimes.com/2012/05/08/business/global/new-ambitions-in-philippine-film-business.html?pagewanted=all

Chapter 8. Filipinos to Know
1. Nickie Wang, "Introducing Fernando Amorsolo to a new generation." *Manila Standard Today*, September 13, 2008. http://andronico.wordpress.com/2008/09/13/introducing-fernando-amorsolo-to-a-new-generation/
2. Pico Iyer, "Woman of the Year." *Time*, January 5, 1987. http://content.time.com/time/subscriber/article/0,33009,963185,00.html
3. Harry Balais, "The Josefa Llanes Escoda Museum." LegendHarry: Your Philippines 101 Guide.http://harrybalais.com/travels/the-josefa-llanes-escoda-museum/
4. "The Magsaysay Award: History." Ramon Magsaysay Award Foundation. http://www.rmaf.org.ph/home.php?id=2&page=history
5. Lennox Lewis, "Heroes & Icons: Manny Pacquiao," The 2009 Time 100. Time, April 30, 2009.http://content.time.com/time/specials/packages/article/0,28804,1894410_1894289_1894356,00.html

Books

Burgan, Michael. *Philippines: Countries Around the World.* Chicago: Heinemann Library, 2012.

Franchino, Vicky. *It's Cool to Learn About Countries: Philippines.* North Mankato, Minn.: Cherry Lake Publishing, 2010.

Schraff, Anne. *Philippines (Country Explorers).* Minneapolis: Lerner Publications, 2009.

Scog, Jason. *Teens in the Philippines (Global Connetions).* North Mankato, Minn.: Compass Point Books, 2008.

Sheen, Barbara. *Foods of the Philippines (A Taste of Culture).* San Diego, Calif.: Kidhaven, 2006.

Tope, Lily Rose and Detch Nonan-Mercado. *Philippines: Cultures of the World.* Tarrytown, New York: Benchmark Books, 2002.

On the Internet

BBCNature News: First wild images of rare mammals (spotted deer)
    http://www.bbc.co.uk/nature/17832277
BBC Nature: Tarsiers
    http://www.bbc.co.uk/nature/life/Tarsier
The Philippines: Children's Corner, presented by the (Philippines) National Commission for the Government and the Arts
    http://www.ncca.gov.ph/pambata/childrenscorner.htm

WORKS CONSULTED

Books

Belliveau, Denis, and Francis Donnell. *In the Footsteps of Marco Polo.* Lanham, Maryland: Rowman & Littlefield , 2008.

De Witt Willcox, Cornelis. *The Head Hunters of Northern Luzon.* Kansas City, Missouri: Franklin Hudson,1912. http://www.gutenberg.org/files/12970/12970-h/12970-h.htm

Halili, Christine N. *Philippine History.* Manila: Rex Book Store, 2004.

Jennings, Ralph. *Insight Guides: Philippines.* London: Insight Guides, 2013.

Osborne, Milton E. *Exploring Southeast Asia: A Traveller's History of the Region.* Crows Nest, Australia: Allen & Unwin, 2002.

Roces, Alfredo and Grace Roces. *Culture Shock: Philippines.* Portland, Oregon: Graphic Arts Center Publishing Company, 2001.

Tarling, N. *The Cambridge History of Southeast Asia.* Cambridge, United Kingdom: Cambridge University Press, 2008.

Williams, China. *Southeast Asia on a Shoestring.* 15th ed. Footscray, Australia: Lonely Planet, 2010.

Periodicals and Newspapers

Cruz, Elfren S. "Cory's legacy of leadership." *Philippine Star,* August 1, 2013.
    http://www.philstar.com/opinion/2013/08/01/1037511/corys-legacy-leadership
Iyer, Pico. "Woman of the Year." *Time,* January 5, 1987. http://content.time.com/time/subscriber/article/0,33009,963185,00.html
Jarque, Edu. "Panagbenga Festival 2013: Seeing stars among the flowers." *The Philippine Star,* March 7, 2013. http://www.philstar.com/entertainment/2013/03/07/916672/panagbenga-festival-2013-seeing-stars-among-flowers
Lewis, Lennox. "Heroes & Icons: Manny Pacquiao," The 2009 Time 100. *Time,* April 30, 2009. http://content.time.com/time/specials/packages/article/0,28804,1894410_1894289_1894356,00.html
Loeb, Vernon. "Natives Who Worship Pinatubo Feel Its Wrath." *Seattle Times,* July 21, 1991. http://community.seattletimes.nwsource.com/archive/?date=19910721&slug=1295627

"Mt. Pinatubo's cloud shades global climate," *Science News*, July 18, 1992.
http://www.thefreelibrary.com/
Mt.+Pinatubo%27s+cloud+shades+global+climate.-a012467057

O'Donnell, Michelle. "Cardinal Jaime Sin, a Champion of the Poor in the Philippines, Is Dead at 76." *New York Times*, June 21, 2005. http://www.nytimes.com/2005/06/21/obituaries/21sin.html

Wang, Nickie. "Introducing Fernando Amorsolo to a new generation." *Manila Standard Today*, September 13, 2008. http://andronico.wordpress.com/2008/09/13/introducing-fernando-amorsolo-to-a-new-generation/

Whaley, Floyd. "New Ambitions in Philippine Film Business." *New York Times*, May 7, 2012. http://www.nytimes.com/2012/05/08/business/global/new-ambitions-in-philippine-film-business.html?pagewanted=all

On the Internet

"1934-1964: War and Independence," PBS Frontline: A Conflicted Land—Rebellion, Wars, and Insurgencies in the Philippines. http://www.pbs.org/frontlineworld/stories/philippines/tl02.html

"7 Fantastic Festivals in the Philippines You Shouldn't Miss," HubPages.com.
http://literarygeisha.hubpages.com/hub/7-fantastic-festivals-in-the-philippines

"Ati-Atigan: a guide to the Philippines' exultant 800 year old festival." LonelyPlanet.com: "Philippines," July 27, 2012. http://www.lonelyplanet.com/philippines/travel-tips-and-articles/76270

Ati-Atihan Festival
http://www.kaliboatiatihan.ph/Ati-Atihan/about-kalibo-ati-atihan.html

Balais, Harry. "The Josefa Llanes Escoda Museum." LegendHarry: Your Philippines 101 Guide. http://harrybalais.com/travels/the-josefa-llanes-escoda-museum/

Bara, Hannbal. "The History of the Muslim in the Philippines." Sub-commission on Cultural Communities and Traditional Arts — (the Philippines) National Commission for Culture and the Arts. 2011. http://www.ncca.gov.ph/about-culture-and-arts/articles-on-c-n-a/article.php?igm=4&i=232

Bataan Death March
http://www.bataanmarch.com/r09/history.htm

"The Battle of Mactan. Lapu Lapu Versus Magellan." Mactan.com
http://lapulapu.weebly.com

Destruction of the USS Maine - Department of the Navy
http://www.history.navy.mil/faqs/faq71-1.htm

Earthquakes
http://earthquake.usgs.gov/earthquakes/eqarchives/year/byyear.php

"Emilio Aguinaldo: Biography." Biography.com
http://www.biography.com/people/emilio-aguinaldo-9177563

Esmula, Wadja and Muhiddin Batara Mutia. "Islam in the Philippines." Islam and Muslims in the Philippines. http://www.islamawareness.net/Asia/Philippines/philippines.html

"Festivals," Ethnic Groups of the Philippines
http://www.ethnicgroupsphilippines.com/people/ethnic-groups-in-the-philippines/ilongot/

Festivals

The Magsaysay Award: History." Ramon Magsaysay Award Foundation.
http://www.rmaf.org.ph/home.php?id=2&page=history

San Augustin Church
http://sanagustinchurch.org/index.php

GLOSSARY

catalyst (CAA-tuh-list)—An action that brings about a change.

colony (KAWL-uh-nee)—A geographic area ruled by a foreign country, usually one that is far away.

galleon (GAL-ee-uhn)—A large Spanish sailing ship with several masts and two or three decks.

habitat (HAA-buh-tat)—Area or environment where a plant or animal lives and grows.

junk (JUNK)—Chinese ship with bamboo masts, often used to transport goods.

magnitude (MAG-nuh-tood)—The size and extent of something.

palettes (PAAL-uhts)—Ranges of colors.

sanctioned (SANK-shunned)—Authorized, given official permission.

scimitar (SIHM-uh-tahr)—Curved sword that broadens toward the tip.

stratosphere (STRAA-tuhs-fear)—Area of the earth's atmosphere starting at 4 to 11 miles (6.5 to 18 kilometers) above the Earth's surface (depending on latitude) and extending up to 30 miles (50 kilometers).

sulfuric acid (suhl-FUHR-ik AA-sihd)—A very strong, corrosive acid.

typhoon (tie-FOON)—Pacific storm with strong winds and high waves; known as a hurricane in the Atlantic area.

valedictorian (vaal-uh-dik-TOHR-ee-uhn)—Person with the highest grades in a graduating class.

PHOTO CREDITS: Cover–Photos.com; p. 1–Daniel Braun/Flickr/Getty Images; pp. 2–3–John Harper/Photodisc/Getty Images; pp. 2, 3, 6–7, 8, 10, 11, 26, 56–Photos.com; pp. 7, 15, 16, 24, 28, 30, 49, 50–cc-by-sa; p. 23-Dennis M. Sabangan/EPA/Newscom; p. 13–Richard P. Hoblitt/U.S. Geological Survey; p. 14–University of Texas at Austin, Perry-Castañeda Library Map Collection; p. 20–National Historical Commission of the Philippines; p. 33–Library of Congress, LC-DIG-hec-12736; pp. 34–35, 36, 38–National Archives & Records Administration; pp. 39, 53–Philippine Presidential Museum and Library; p. 41–Bettmann/Corbis/AP Images; p. 42–AP Images; p. 44–Rome Gacad/AFP/Getty Images/Newscom; p. 46–Mark Navales/AFP/Getty Images/Newscom; p. 47–Dirck Halstead/Getty Images; p. 48–Alexander Tamargo/Getty Images; p. 55–Gene Blevins/ZUMAPress/Newscom. Every effort has been made to locate all copyright holders of material used in this book. If any errors or omissions have occurred, corrections will be made in future editions of the book.

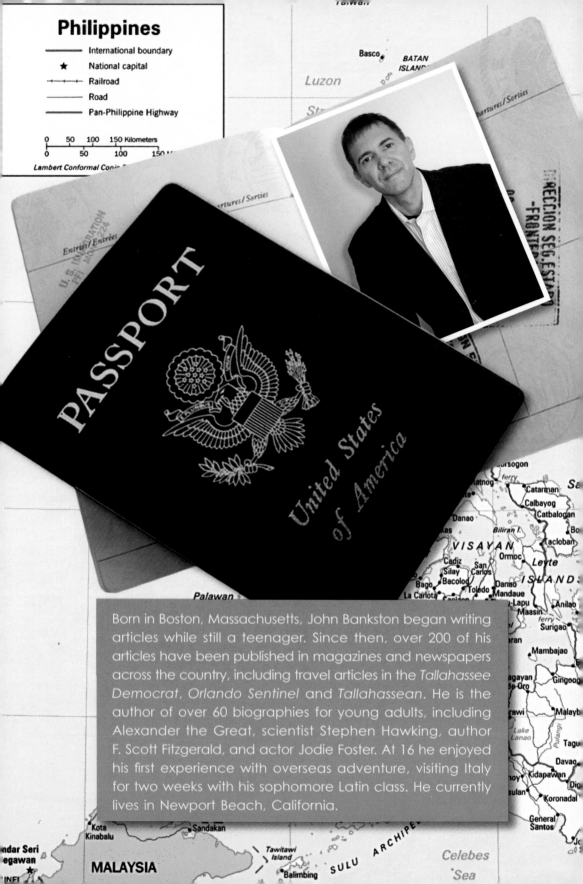

Philippines

— International boundary
★ National capital
⊢⊣⊢⊣ Railroad
—— Road
—— Pan-Philippine Highway

| 0 | 50 | 100 | 150 Kilometers |
| 0 | 50 | 100 | 150 M |

Lambert Conformal Conic

Born in Boston, Massachusetts, John Bankston began writing articles while still a teenager. Since then, over 200 of his articles have been published in magazines and newspapers across the country, including travel articles in the *Tallahassee Democrat*, *Orlando Sentinel* and *Tallahassean*. He is the author of over 60 biographies for young adults, including Alexander the Great, scientist Stephen Hawking, author F. Scott Fitzgerald, and actor Jodie Foster. At 16 he enjoyed his first experience with overseas adventure, visiting Italy for two weeks with his sophomore Latin class. He currently lives in Newport Beach, California.